Whittling
Twigs
and
Branches

by Chris Lubkemann

Fox
Chapel Publishing

1970 Broad Street • East Petersburg, PA 17520
www.FoxChapelPublishing.com

The first edition of *Whittling Twigs and Branches* was a greatly expanded combination of the author's two self-published books, *Carving Twigs and Branches* and *More Carving Twigs and Branches*. This second edition includes two new step-by-step demonstrations on whittling a flower and whittling a letter opener, expanded painting and finishing information, instructions for adding a base, instructions for creating hens and chicks, tips for correcting mistakes and additional gallery photos.

ISBN: 978-1-56523-236-5
Library of Congress Control Number: 2004102185

Publisher's Cataloging-in-Publication Data

Lubkemann, Ernest C.

Whittling twigs and branches / by Chris Lubkemann. -- 2nd ed .--
East Petersburg, PA : Fox Chapel Publishing, c2004.

p. ; cm.

ISBN: 978-1-56523-236-5 ; 1-56523-263-4
"Unique birds, flowers, trees & more from easy-to-find wood" --
Cover.

1. Wood-carving. 2. Twigs. I. Title.

TT199.7. L8223 2004   2004102185
736/.4--dc22   2008

To learn more about the other great books from Fox Chapel Publishing,
or to find a retailer near you, call toll-free 800-457-9112
or visit us at **www.FoxChapelPublishing.com**.

Note to Authors: We are always looking for talented authors to write new books
in our area of woodworking, design, and related crafts. Please send a brief letter describing your idea to
Acquisition Editor, 1970 Broad Street, East Petersburg, PA 17520.

Printed in China
10 9 8 7 6 5 4

Table of Contents

Chris Lubkemann, of Lancaster, Pennsylvania, was born of missionary parents in Brazil and remembers his earliest attempts at woodcarving in the Ucayali River town of Contamana, deep in the Amazon rain forest of eastern Peru. Strangely enough, that first whittling project when he was around seven years old consisted of an assortment of little wooden dentist tools! His dentistry career was very short-lived, though, as his mom thought it probably wasn't the best idea for jungle kids to be poking around in each other's mouths.

His appreciation for wood and love for making things from it never stopped. There were boats, bows and arrows, doll furniture, slingshots and treehouses. His first forked-branch rooster hatched in the summer of 1966, between his junior and senior years of college. Dr. John Luke, a longtime and very loved minister in the mountains of northwestern North Carolina, showed Chris in a few minutes how a rooster could emerge from a Y-shaped branch. As things turned out, Chris ended up whittling away quite a few hours of that '66–'67 academic year to actually help pay for it! And he had lots of fun in the process, too.

Chris Lubkemann

Together with his wife, Sheri, and three children, Chris served in Portugal from 1972 to 1986, followed by a U.S.-based ministry that has taken him to a number of foreign countries as well as different parts of the United States. Wherever he has gone, he's always had a pocketknife or two at hand and a handful of twigs and branches, and for quite a few years now his airline carry-on "bag" has consisted of one or another of his wooden display cases. So, the simple craft picked up more than 40 years ago in the mountains of Ashe County, North Carolina, keeps getting shared and passed on to folks all over, and the number of branch carvers worldwide continues to grow!

Getting Started

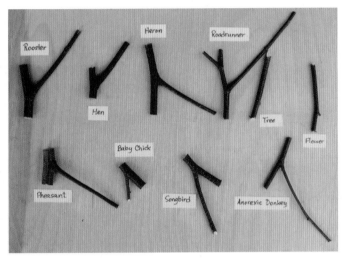

The beginnings of a number of different projects. One of the best parts about carving twig and branch projects is that the basic raw material is free.

Branch and twig whittling or carving is a very satisfying hobby. And, if the whole story is told, it can be far more than a hobby—a fun way to help buy groceries, pay school bills, pay off the mortgage and contribute toward meeting other expenses that come along.

All this can happen with almost no cash outlay. Other than the small amount of money needed to buy a knife, a few brushes, a little bit of paint and glue and little more, there's practically nothing else to buy. The basic raw material—twigs and branches—is free. And it's a craft that can be done just about anywhere. There's no need for fancy dust collectors or protective face masks. Electricity is needed mostly for the light bulb illuminating the work station. A little bit of time and a dose of focused concentration are all you need to learn to whittle twigs and branches into wonderful creations.

A Word about Knives

The basic tool for carving the great majority of the projects suggested in the following pages is a very sharp knife. Technically, I guess I should say a couple of very sharp blades. As for the handles to which these blades are connected, that's a matter of personal preference or practicality. The blade could be part of a standard folding pocketknife or set into a traditional fixed-blade carving knife. Having worked with many folks in the woodcarving community, I've seen very good branch carvings produced with fixed-blade knives. To be honest, however, my own preference is still a good old-fashioned two-blade pocketknife. I always have one in my pocket, and it's ready to go at a moment's notice.

And you won't believe all the unusual places and situations where that pocketknife has come out and started moving chips and shavings around! Banquets, wedding receptions, commencement exercises, airplanes, trains, boats, buses, cars, dentist chairs, doctors' offices, hospitals, all kinds of sporting events, living rooms, kitchens, backyards, front yards, baseball ticket lines...and even in the voting line during the most recent presidential election! And these are only some of the impromptu, informal whittling venues in which I have carved. The formal, scheduled ones have been many and varied too, and they include seminars at carving clubs, classes at adult education sites and demonstrations for scouts.

Whatever your preference regarding knife handles, you'll need two good, sharp blades: One should be fairly small, no longer than $1^1/_2$ inches long, and the other should be larger, between 2 and $2^1/_2$ inches. Over the years, I've used quite a few different pocketknives. I have been well-served by my Victorinox Swiss Army Tinker and recommend it highly. I've also used the slightly smaller Victorinox Recruit in my workshops and it works very well. The Victorinox Hiker is essentially the same knife as the Tinker, with an excellent saw blade added. The saw can prove to be extremely useful in harvesting branches if you don't have pruning shears handy.

If you are using a two-blade pocketknife, most of your whittling will be done with the small blade. **(See Illustration 1a.)** I've found, in many cases, it is often necessary to taper the smaller blade down somewhat to give it the ideal shape. This is especially important for accurate small radius cuts. After the blade has been tapered down, it should be resharpened and honed.

The knife I always carry with me—and use—is a simple, two-blade pocketknife, probably not what most people think of as the standard carving tool. Of the nine knives on this stump, the third one from the left, the Victorinox Tinker Swiss Army Knife, and the one at the far right, a "cheapie but goodie" by Imperial, are two I've used the most. I figure my Tinker has been involved in about $120,000 worth of carvings as of this writing. Not bad for a $20 knife.

Illustration 1a
The shape of the small blade of most pocketknives is somewhat like the shape illustrated by the solid line. You'll have a much more useful blade if its shape follows the pattern indicated by the broken line. The tip will make tighter turns.

The large blade of the average new pocketknife usually needs to be reworked to get it into the best shape for making curls. The factory-sharpened edge is generally too "wedgy." Those little corners need to be taken off, leaving a slightly curved "shoulder." **(See Illustration 1b.)** A perfectly **flat** bevel on the larger blade will not allow the blade to produce

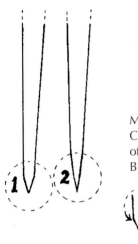

Magnified
Cross-Section
of Large
Blade

Illustration 1b
The factory edge of most pocketknives is illustrated by Figure 1. Sharpen the blade to conform to Figure 2, getting rid of the corners.

decent curls when slicing the feathers of the rooster's tail. One reason even so many experienced carvers have difficulty getting a good curled tail on a rooster is that most fixed-blade carving knives (which most of them are using) have very long, flat bevels with practically no "shoulder" at all to help curl the feather as it's sliced. If you have several fixed-blade knives and they are what you prefer to use, I'd suggest taking one of them and working it into the shape suggested in Illustration 1b. That will be your "curl" blade.

Sharpening and Honing

There are at least several ways to reshape your blade and to do the primary sharpening. Some carvers use sharpening stones; others might use a fairly fine file; still others have special sharpening or grinding wheels. It doesn't really matter what system you use to get the knife blade into a good basic shape for branch carving—as long as you do get it done.

As I look back on my own history of shaping and sharpening blades, I recall using all of these methods and others at different times. The particular system I use depends, more or less, on what's available at the moment. My very old, very worn two-sided sharpening stone has been my most common tool

Reshaping Your Pocketknife

For what it's worth, let me walk you through the steps I take to transform a Victorinox Swiss Army Tinker into an ideal branch-carving pocketknife.

1. The Tinker as it comes from the box.

2. Remove the key ring and saw off the little tab that holds it. File off any sharp edges. (I remove this tab because it is located in exactly the wrong place if you're going to use the small blade a lot, especially the way you do in carving.)

3. Taper the small blade top and bottom to bring the blade to a thinner point, which is much better for tighter turn cuts. Notice the difference between the small blades in Step 1 and Step 3. Now you'll have to resharpen and hone the small blade.

I might mention that the Victorinox Swiss Army knives are among the few pocketknives that I've found to be reasonably sharp right out of the box. However, I'm sure most carvers will want to fine-tune both blades to get the edge they find ideal.

And one further note: I would not recommend any of the knives with the corkscrew, as the corkscrew makes for a very uncomfortable grip when working with the small blade. The Phillips screwdriver of the Tinker nestles quite nicely into the handle and doesn't bother you the way the corkscrew does.

for my basic reshaping and sharpening, because it is usually what I have on hand. Experiment and choose the system that works best for you.

A honing device may be one of any number of devices, or a combination of several different ones. Use whatever helps you to get a really sharp blade. My own very simple, but effective system consists of several strips of wet-or-dry sandpaper or emery cloth glued or held to a thin strip of wood. The more worn down the strips of sandpaper are, the better they hone and polish the blade. I'm sure I've used some of my strips for at least five years! The three grits of wet-or-dry sandpaper I use are #320, #400 and #600. Of course, some of my old pieces would probably now be classified as #5000! The back side of an old leather belt has also served me well as a strop. You can also purchase a honing device from mail order woodworking catalogs or your local woodcarving supply store.

Sharpening and Honing Tips

I have never measured the precise angle to which I sharpen my blades, but I do know that I keep the blade fairly flat against the stone or sandpaper. My smaller blades have a flatter taper than my larger blades. Remember, the larger blade is the one that will be used to carve the curled feathers and therefore needs to have at least some "shoulder."

On each surface, I start out with a circular motion and end up with a number of slicing strokes, slicing into the blade. If my knife is already sharp and just needs a little touch, I'll do this procedure on the finest, most-worn strip of sandpaper. If the blade is dull, I'll start with the 320-grit paper and go progressively finer until the blade is truly sharp.

I end up with a few strops on my little belt strip, heading away from the cutting edge. This is where you might choose to use some of the honing sticks and compounds that are available from various woodcarving supply sources.

The system just described is quite simple and super-cheap, but it works! Once you get the hang of it, you'll love it and just might end up using it on your kitchen knives, too.

Other Supplies

The other supplies and tools you need will depend largely on how you decide to finish your projects.

Paint: Choose acrylics or enamels that are thick enough not to run or bleed. Start with red, yellow and black. I prefer a spice red and a slightly orange yellow.

Brushes: Keep several sizes ranging from #00 or #0 to #2 or #3 on hand. Use a larger size for applying liquid finish. I've found that it's not necessary to buy the most expensive brushes, but neither does it pay to purchase the cheapest ones.

Finish: For some projects or parts of projects almost any finish will work—shellac, varnish or any type of polyurethane. However, for finishing a rooster with a nicely curled tail, make sure you use an oil-based polyurethane or other synthetic finish that won't straighten out the tail feathers. Alcohol-based shellacs or water-based polyurethanes tend to uncurl the feathers, especially on days when the relative humidity is high. Certain clear acrylic spray finishes work well if they are not overdone.

Glue: Yellow carpenter's glue works very well to glue the carved figures into bases or settings. This kind of glue can also mend a broken beak or weak tail feather! Liquid cyanoacrylate glue (also called CA glue or Super Glue™) is a great reinforcing agent when it is allowed to soak into ruffled neck feathers, branches of a miniature tree, petals of tiny flowers and other very fine or delicate shavings.

Characteristics of Good Wood

One of the most frequently asked questions I've heard over the years has been, "What kind of wood do you use?" To be perfectly honest, the longer I'm around wood (and the people who work with it), the more I learn; and the more I learn and share, the more I realize how little I really know and how much more there is to learn!

The more you work with twigs and branches, the more you'll develop a quick eye for the best kinds to use and the most likely places to find them. And if you keep your eyes open, you'll find great raw material even in some of the most unlikely places. A number of years ago during an unexpected 24-hour layover in Japan, I was walking along a path outside the hotel and found several little branches lying on the ground. I don't have the slightest clue as to what kind of wood they were, but they worked! Then there was a road-side trash pile that produced a special piece, which I wholesaled for $250, as well as one of my all-time favorite Dr. Seuss-type characters. Yep, there are all kinds of wood in all sorts of places just waiting for some creative carver to pass by and whittle them into shape!

First let me suggest some specific characteristics to look for in an ideal branch, as well as a few general guidelines I've found helpful. Then I'll list a number of specific types of wood I've carved and make a few comments about my own experience with them.

Freshness/Dryness of Branches

There definitely is a trick or two in hitting the best time window for producing a good tail. The body (all except the tail) can be carved when the fork is still quite fresh. Keep in mind, however, that wet or green wood will not curl on its own as it is shaved or thinly sliced. I think I can say quite accurately that it is virtually impossible to get a really good natural curl if the wood is damp or wet, no matter how sharp your blade is or how thin you make the individual feather slices. Wet or damp wood may *curve* a bit, but it will not *curl* by itself as it is sliced.

Keep in mind that it is the varying degrees of wetness and dryness that allow the wood to curl as you carve. If you're carving a rooster, you'll want drier wood for more curl. If you're carving a pheasant or a heron, you'll want to work with fresher wood for less curl. So, if you're working with a freshly cut wood fork, stop after carving the rooster's body and let the already debarked tail branch dry a bit before carving the feathers.

The exact amount of time you wait will depend on the type of wood, air temperature, atmospheric humidity and thickness of the branch. Some very thin branches will need to dry for only 20 to 30 min-

utes after the bark is removed. Others may need to dry for an hour or two. You may even need to let a thicker tail branch dry overnight. Whatever you do, however, don't let the debarked tail branch dry out completely, especially if you're working with something like live oak, swamp maple or black birch. If you do, you'll end up with a fight on your hands trying to get tail feathers out of a rock-hard branch!

For most figures, it is definitely best to avoid wood that is so dry that the branch snaps cleanly in two when bent. I prefer carving a branch that is reasonably fresh or at least has some moisture still in it. This could be anything from a branch that has just recently been pruned to one cut from a tree that blew down several months previously and has been slowly drying. A lot, of course, depends on the type of wood. Generally speaking, I've found the best branches for carving are neither just freshly cut nor very dry.

Some of the hardwoods, such as various maples, oaks and beech, need to be worked when they're still quite fresh. Other branches—linden, for example—can be carved when they are much more seasoned. Some of the birches—with the notable exception of black birch, which is harder than other varieties—can also be carved nicely when they've dried out quite a bit. This is especially true for some of the very thin birch twigs used for carving the smallest miniatures.

To keep branches from drying out too much, I cut them up into ready-to-carve forks and store them in plastic bags in the freezer. Of course this assumes that you can negotiate with your family's freezer administrator for wood storage space! (Some carvers actually sneak dead birds into the freezer—maybe even frogs and lizards—so some nice, clean, packaged twigs and branches shouldn't be too difficult to squeeze in!)

I've been asked if it's possible to soak branches that have become too hard and too dry. Actually, I have done that. I then treat the wood fork as if it were a freshly-cut branch, letting it re-dry some before working it. One problem I've sometimes found with soaking certain woods, however, is that the bark

Illustration 1c
The pith at the center of an ideal branch should be very small. A branch ¹/₂ inch in diameter should have a pith no greater than ¹/₁₆ inch in diameter.

Illustration 1d
The grain of a forked branch runs in three different directions—ideal for branch carving.

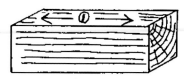

Illustration 1e
The grain in a block of wood runs in one direction.

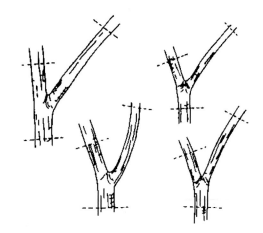

Illustration 1f
The ideal branch has no knots in the wood between the dotted lines. Knots can make branch carving difficult, but not impossible.

can loosen and deteriorate. In any case, my own branch-carving philosophy has been more or less: "Don't make more work for yourself than you have to. When you can work with an ideal branch, do!" Of course, if you find yourself in the middle of the Mohave Desert and all you have is a little, bone-dry twig, I'm sure you'll find a way to make it work, even if the whole process takes five times as long as usual!

Generally, I avoid using wood that forces me to deal with a lot of sticky sap. This is one of the reasons I rarely use pine branches. If I carved fresh pine, I'd be spending an awful lot of time cleaning my knife and my hands!

Hardness/Softness of Wood

Of the 80 or so kinds of wood I've carved in the past 37 years, the vast majority have been hard woods. Even some of the hardest, such as live oak, water oak and ironwood, work very well when they're fairly fresh. Some softer woods, such as linden, can carve well, although I've found that the softer woods tend to have a large pith, especially in the smaller branches.

The pith is that small, soft area at the center of a branch. The ideal branch for carving has a relatively small pith. Ideally a branch that is ¹/₂ inch in diameter shouldn't have a pith that is more than ¹/₁₆ inch thick. **(See Illustration 1c.)**

The Ideal Wood Fork

Because of a wood fork's shape, the grain of the wood runs in three directions from the center of the Y. **(See Illustration 1d.)** This feature creates structural strength and results in a final project that is relatively strong, yet flexible, and not easily broken in spite of its delicate appearance. Because of its natural formation, there are some things you can do with a forked branch that you could never do with even the most perfect block of wood because the grain in that block runs in only one direction. **(See Illustration 1e.)**

For most branch figures, I think you'll find it a lot easier to work with a wood fork that is free of knots inside the areas marked by the dotted lines. **(See Illustration 1f.)** In time, you'll discover that knots and extra branches in certain locations inside these lines don't significantly affect the carving. They may just make the project more challenging, but not impossible.

A silver maple tree cut down by an Amish farmer will provide many twigs for hours of carving.

Nicely forked twigs can come from a variety of trees.

I found many ideal branches for twig carvings on these limbs lopped off of my neighbor's birch tree.

Most figures I carve come from branches less than one inch in diameter. A good-sized fork for beginning twig carvers should have a main stem with a diameter of $1/2$ to $3/4$ inch. A lot of people think that a great big, thick, wood fork is the easiest fork to carve for their first rooster. Not really! Tails on a thick branch can put up a pretty good fight and make you sweat bullets! And don't be afraid to try the smaller branches ($1/4$ to $1/2$ inch in diameter). They're easier to work and can be all kinds of fun. Now, when you start carving really little twigs ($1/8$-inch-thick or less) the challenge starts to grow again.

When to Cut Branches

For the most part, I've found that any time of the year is a good time to cut wood. Even winter is great because it's easy to spot the best-shaped branches. And if you happen to be tramping through a frozen-over New Jersey swamp looking for a swamp maple (which, by the way, grows in a lot of places besides swamps), you can walk on solid footing. Another cold-weather advantage is that if you're branch hunting in rattlesnake or cottonmouth country, the snakes are asleep! That's definitely a plus! In the summer it's not a bad idea to keep one eye looking for branches and the other eye on the lookout for...well, whatever might be crawling nearby.

Wood Species

Naturally, some varieties of wood work better than others, but it's not always possible to have the ideal wood fork at hand. Just experiment with the kinds of branches you collect. Chances are pretty good that you'll find at least one kind of tree or bush that does the trick, and before long, you'll develop your own list of favorite raw materials. Some trees yield a good carving fork at just about every intersection or Y. Birch trees are among the very best. I also fondly remember the lentisco bushes in Portugal as another A+ wood. In other trees, you may have to hunt quite a bit to find the best-shaped forks.

Two of the largest trees in Lancaster County used to be in my front yard. Imagine the number of branches for carving on these American elms! Sadly, since this photo was taken, these two beautiful trees succumbed to a combination of blights and are in the process of being taken down. However, some of the branches, superbly carved just under the bark by a myriad of little critters, are now slated to become lamps, stools, tables and who knows what else down the road.

Birch: As I've said, among the very best! All of the varieties of birch I've used have been good. Black birch is quite a bit harder than the other birches. One little quirk about birch is that when you slice the tail feathers, you may find your knife blade sort of "catching" on the wood and you may hear a squeaking sound. Birch is one of only two or three types of wood I've ever carved that does this.

Maple: Some are better than others because they have a smaller pith. Swamp maple is one of my favorites.

Oak: As with maple, some oaks work better than others, but don't let the fact that oaks in general are very hard keep you from trying this wood.

Willow: Weeping willow tends to be a bit brittle, but some of the other varieties of willow work well.

Elm: Guaranteed to have a lot of nicely shaped forks.

Beech: A very hard wood that forks out beautifully. The wood looks green when you first cut it but soon changes to more of a white.

Cherry: I've carved different kinds of cherry. The wood itself is nice to carve, but I've found that the bark of wild cherry sometimes tends to wrinkle and separate from the branch as it dries.

Cedar: In spite of some sap with which to contend, cedar produces some beautiful pieces. It tends to be a little more brittle than some other woods, so be careful as you make the vertical cuts on the rooster's comb so as not to split the wood.

Orange, Tangerine, Grapefruit, Lemon (Citrus): Some more of my favorites. All very hard, but excellent woods. If you live in citrus country, orchard-pruning time is a great time to find wood.

Apple, Pear, Peach, Plum: While these fruit trees don't produce the best carving forks, I have managed to carve some fairly decent pieces from them.

Flowering Plum, Flowering Crabapple: Hard woods, nicely shaped forks, pretty colors.

Sycamore: Good for larger roosters; quite hard with an interesting grain.

Redbud: I first tried redbud in Statesville, North Carolina, when I missed my turn onto I-77 and had to drive a few blocks farther in order to turn around. I ended up making a left onto a street that had a whole pile of freshly pruned branches lying alongside the road. The redbud branches worked well. (Thank God for some of the "missed turns" in life!)

Holly: A very clear, straight-grained wood. I use different varieties of holly.

Olive: Good forks, somewhat slower drying than most woods.

Guava: Not too many of us have guava trees in our backyards, but for those who do…carve away. I've made some very good carvings from quince too.

Indian Rosewood, Bottlebrush, Viburnum: Some good woods I've used in Florida.

Alnos: A very good wood I used while visiting the Philippines.

Hedge Bushes: I've used a fair number of different ones, though I don't have the slightest clue what kind they are! Some have very nice forks.

The Basics of Making Curls

In each of the chapters that follow, we will go through the steps of carving roosters, hens and chicks, pheasants, herons, roadrunners, trees, flowers and letter openers. Many carvers, with just those explanations, will go on to master the curling techniques and even develop a new trick or two of their own. For what it's worth, let me just share with you some strokes and techniques I've learned in the past 37 years.

Ten Rules for Branch Carving

People who don't succeed at branch carving usually fail for one of two reasons (and often both): 1) Their knives are not sharp, or 2) they don't follow directions carefully. So...

1. Make sure your knife is sharp.
2. **Make sure your knife is sharp.**
3. Make sure your knife is sharp.
4. Make sure your knife is sharp.
5. *Make sure your knife is sharp.*
6. Make sure your knife is sharp.
7. Make SURE your knife is sharp.
8. MAKE SURE YOUR KNIFE IS SHARP.
9. MAKE SURE YOUR KNIFE IS SHARP!!!
10. Follow the directions carefully...

...at least at first! There are some places in the step-by-step process where two steps can be done in reverse order, but generally speaking I have organized the steps in a way that will keep you from messing up a step you've already completed.

Basic Cutting Strokes

There are several ways to use a knife. The three particular strokes described here are illustrated for right-handed carvers. Lefties, of course, will reverse the hands, following a mirror image of the illustrations.

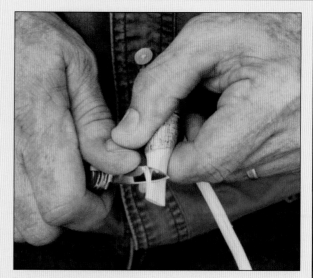

Straightaway Cutting

This cut is good for removing a lot of wood or bark quickly. Hold the wood in your left hand and, using long strokes, cut away from yourself with your right hand. I find that when I use this stroke my right wrist is pretty well locked.

Thumbpushing

This particular stroke is extremely practical for small cuts where precise control is needed and you don't want to overcut. Hold the wood in the four fingers of your left hand, leaving your left thumb free. Grip the knife in your right hand, keeping your right thumb against the back of the blade. With your left thumb, push either the back of the blade or the back of your right thumb.

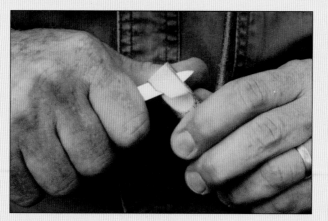

Drawcutting

This technique involves placing the wood in your left hand and the knife in your right. Cut toward yourself (sort of like peeling an orange), with short strokes, using your right thumb as a brace against the wood. Be sure you keep some wood between the blade and your thumb. I find it helpful (and much safer!) to keep my right thumb braced on my left thumb, not on top of the wood itself. That way I don't run the risk of the blade coming up into my right thumb on its follow-through when it suddenly clears the end of the wood.

Curling Cuts

More often than not, beginning branch carvers will do a little "dig" into the branch to get the feather cut started. **(See Illustration 2a.)** Then they'll try to flatten the blade to make the cut down the branch. The truth is, the instant you dig into the branch, you've already started making the tip of the feather too thick, and you've probably ruined the most important part of the curl.

So, do not dig the knife into the wood. Rest the blade against the wood with a firm, steady, **lateral** pressure against the tail branch. Then, holding the knife very firmly for good control, slide the blade **forward** in a **short, slicing** motion. The knife blade itself will lightly "grab" the wood. Then, draw the blade backward, without cutting, and, maintaining the same pressure against the wood, slide/slice forward again. You may repeat this slicing stroke 7-10 times as you cut downward on the branch to make a single feather, dropping only $1/16$ to $1/8$ to $1/4$ of an inch at a time. There's relatively little pressure downward, and most of your concentration is focused on controlling the depth or thickness of the cut. The first several tail feathers especially need to be as thin as possible.

Of course, making feathers this thin can be tricky, and you may lose one or two, or even more. If you do lose a feather, don't worry. Simply smooth the branch and try again from the same point. It is a good idea to always remove the "hump" before beginning the next feather. Carving off this rise gives you a smooth surface for your next feather cut and will keep the tip of the feather thin. **(See Illustration 2b.)**

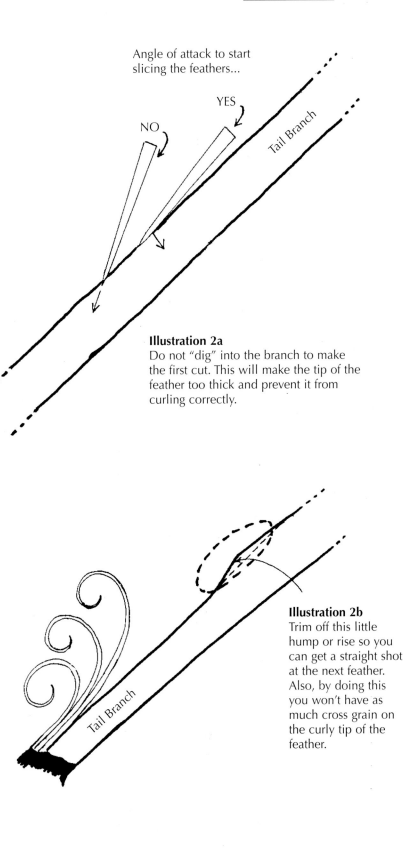

Angle of attack to start slicing the feathers...

NO   YES

Tail Branch

Illustration 2a
Do not "dig" into the branch to make the first cut. This will make the tip of the feather too thick and prevent it from curling correctly.

Illustration 2b
Trim off this little hump or rise so you can get a straight shot at the next feather. Also, by doing this you won't have as much cross grain on the curly tip of the feather.

Tail Branch

Tail Curl How-to

Now let's go through the process with a series of photos. If a picture is really worth a thousand words, the following photos will add another 9,000 or so words to an already long explanation.

There is definitely some know-how involved in deciding when a branch is right for carving. Rooster tails need to be carved when the wood has dried a bit. The dryness of the wood is what allows the feathers to curl as they are cut. Pheasant and roadrunner tails need to be carved when the wood is fresh. The wetness of the wood keeps the branch from curling excessively. (See the section on Freshness/Dryness of Branches in Chapter One for more detailed information.)

Try the following trick to help you decide when a branch is dry enough to carve a rooster tail. When you take the bark off the tail branch of the fork, also remove the bark from another straight branch of the same wood and the same thickness. Use this second branch as a practice and test piece. If the thin slices of the second branch do not curl when you make your cuts, you'll know the wood on the first branch is still too wet for the curling feather cuts of a rooster. If the wood on the second branch curls nicely, the wood on the first branch is also just right for curling. Also, it's not a bad idea to try a few practice tails on this test branch before doing the tail on your almost finished rooster!

1. Starting position. I'm right-handed, so the rooster is resting on my left knee. (Lefties, in my opinion, will do better if they rest the rooster on their right knee.) This position gives better visibility—a good sideways look at the cut. If my head is straight over the cut, I can't easily judge how thick or how thin I'm making the cut.

2. At this point I've probably already made at least two right-to-left cuts (my right to left) with the large blade of my pocketknife and have only sliced about 1/4 inch down the feather. Notice how my hands are braced against my lower chest. This really helps to steady and control the cut.

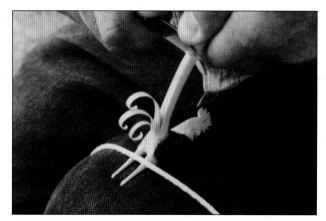

3. Three feathers are done; the fourth is just getting started. Sometimes I find it helpful to use my left thumb against the back of the knife blade to help get the feather cut started.

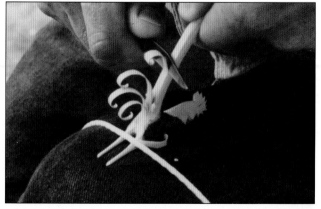

4. Oops! I blew the fourth feather! See it lying on my knee almost on top of the shoelace "vise"? I'll just smooth out the little hump and start another feather. **(See Illustration 2b on page 11.)**

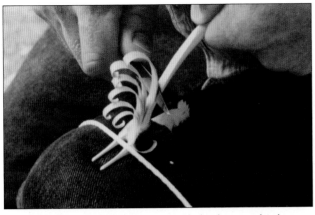

5. A couple of feathers later... Each feather is a bit longer than the previous feather and a bit thicker with less overall curl.

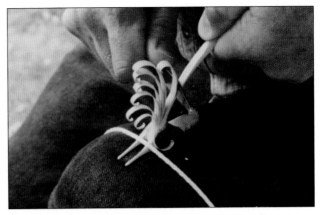

6. Beginning to wind down. With an anticipated two or three feathers left to go, I begin making them successively shorter. This way the end result will give a sort of a fan effect.

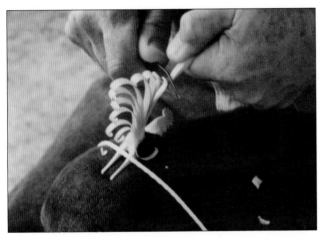

7. Last feather... I cut all the way through the tail branch. Often this last feather will be a bit too thick. If it is, I just thin it by slicing off some wood, cutting upward from the base of the feather toward the tip.

8. Sometimes I may want to bend or kink some of the feathers over the back of my small blade. This might be especially true of the last one or two I've made. I can then separate the feathers and position them exactly where I want them to stay. I don't have to be afraid of bending the feathers. Because they were carved with the grain of the wood, they'll take quite a bit of abuse. Once they're in position, they'll stay there, provided they don't get wet or soaked with a water-based finish.

9. Slice off any little wood hairs or burrs that take away from the smoothness of the feathers. Sometimes this is more easily done after the finish you apply has hardened.

Tail Curl Tricks

The following photos will add an interesting wrinkle or two to your tail-curling cuts—and to the whole concept of branch carving in general. If you are following along with the demonstration, you may have already observed how the angle of your slicing motion affects the direction of the feather's curl. You can add some interesting variety to your carvings by giving these different angles a try.

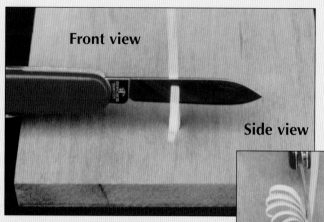

Front view

Side view

Push the knife blade STRAIGHT across the branch, sort of like a perfectly straight plus sign (+). The curl will go straight around in line with the branch.

The knife blade is pointed DOWN as the slices are made. The curls will go to a right-hander's right. (Directions are reversed, of course, for left-handers.)

The knife blade is pointed UP for the same downward strokes. The feather will curl the opposite way.

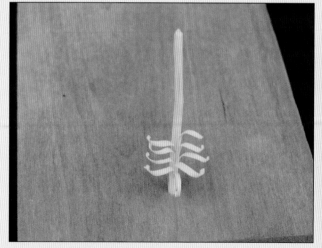

One straight-across cut, followed by alternating downward pointing cuts and upward pointing cuts. Note how the feathers curl in different directions.

Combining a variety of cuts can lead to a rooster tail explosion!

Whittling a Rooster

While the wood fork rooster is definitely not the easiest of all figures to "hatch" from a tree branch, it probably is by far the most popular—sort of the branch-carving mascot! Also, in learning to carve a rooster you will learn most of the basic cuts and techniques that will be used in producing most other projects. Once you have the rooster-carving technique down, it's not that hard to switch over to pheasants, herons, roadrunners and a whole pile of other "critters" and projects.

Forked branches exist in all shapes and sizes, and each rooster you make will be an original, a bit different from every other. The size and shape of the rooster will depend largely on the thickness of the branch and the angle at which the three spokes of the Y meet. Differently shaped wood forks lend themselves naturally to a variety of rooster positions and "personalities." **(See Illustration 3a.)**

A) Pretty much average
B) Leaning forward (looking down) or with head facing totally backward (facing up)
C) Rooster with big, bushy tail
D) Leaning way back, crowing
E) Standing at attention, tail up in the air
F) Very, very discouraged rooster, tail dragging
…And I'm sure you can come up with a lot more!

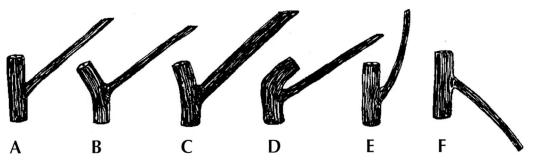

Illustration 3a
The size and shape of a branch-carved rooster depends on the size and shape of the branch.

Rooster Body

Step 1

Cut the wood fork, leaving Branch C 4" or 5" long. For your first rooster, I'd suggest selecting a fork with the bottom branch (Branch B) between 3/8" and 3/4" thick. For a rooster of average proportion, the length of Branch A (head branch) is roughly two times the diameter of the same branch. Length b is slightly greater than length a.

Branch A
(head)

a

b

Branch B
(legs)

Branch C
(tail)

Note: *In carving the rooster, I think you'll find you do a much better job, with much better control, if you use your pocketknife's small blade for all of your carving, except the slicing of the tail feathers in Step 18.*

Step 2

Taper Branch A for the rooster's head and neck. These cuts begin slightly above the bottom of the crotch of the Y. You can vary the direction in which the head is facing. (See the three different views of Branch A, seen from above.)

Branch A
(head)

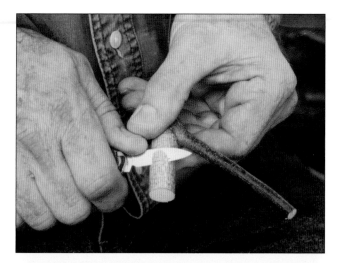

Branch A as seen from above. Vary the cuts to change the position of the head.

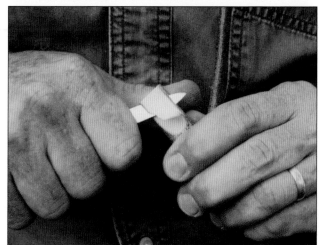

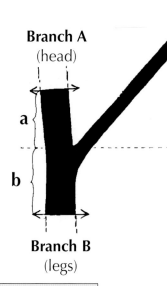

Step 3

Taper Branch B for the rooster's legs. Note that these cuts are curved and that more wood is taken from the front than from the back. This will make the chest puff out more. Notice where these cuts begin in relation to the horizontal dotted line and the bottom of the crotch.

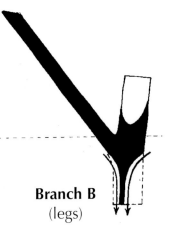

Branch B
(legs)

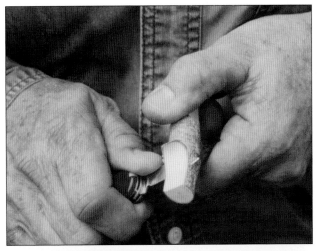

Step 4

Remove the bark from the sides of the tapered Branch B. This is the first step of getting the rooster into his vest.

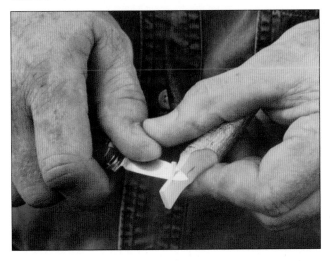

Step 5

Cut the bark off Branches A, B and C, leaving only the rooster's "vest" of natural bark. If you want an all-white rooster—a White Leghorn—you can take off all of the bark. If Branch C is very thick, cut away the bark and some of the wood from the sides.

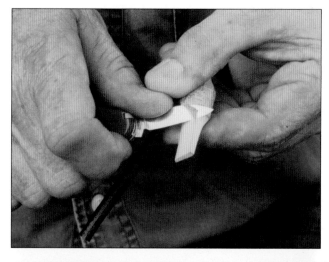

Cross-section of a stripped tail branch with a bit of wood removed from the sides of the branch.

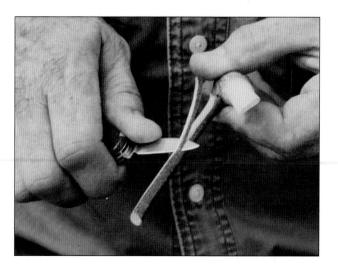

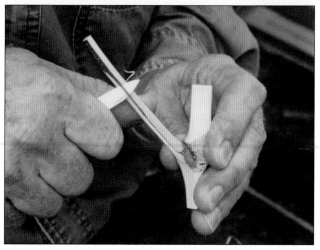

Step 6

Form the legs by cutting away the wood marked by the X. Start at the * with the point of the small blade, cutting in the direction of the arrows, away from the *. (If you try to cut toward the *, you'll discover you will be cutting against the grain, and you'll run a much greater risk of cutting yourself!) Then round and smooth the legs.

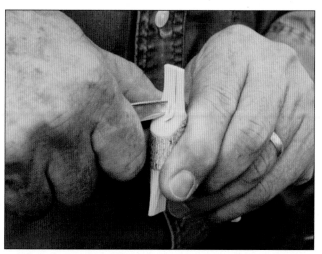

In this photo, I'm holding the rooster upside down. Notice that the blade is facing upward, and the cutting stroke is going away from the * in the drawing.

Step 6 continued

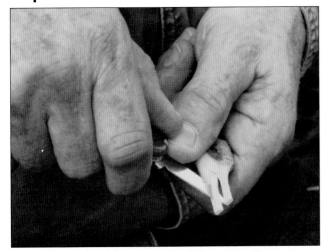

Cutting down the legs, away from the *.

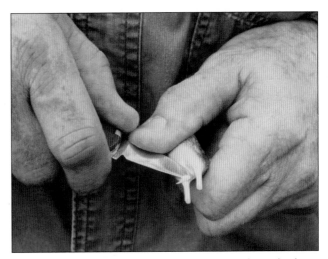

Rounding and smoothing the legs.

Step 7

Cut off a small amount of wood from the front of Branch A (1). Then cut in a slight curve on the top, a bit higher in the back than in the front (2 and 3). On these cuts, make sure you always cut in the direction of the arrows to avoid splitting the wood outward.

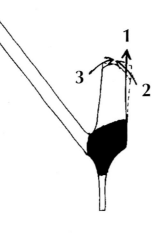

Cut 1

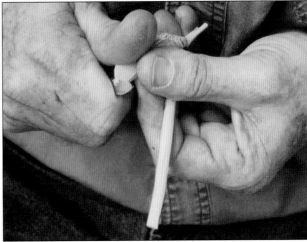

Cut 2

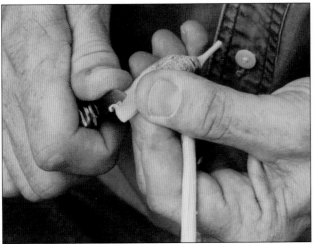

Cut 3

Step 8

Sharpen the top of Branch A for the rooster's comb.

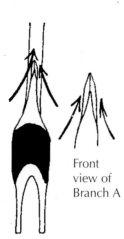

Front view of Branch A

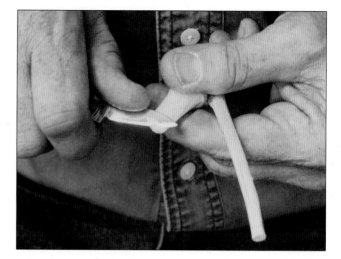

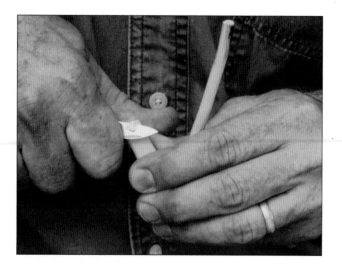

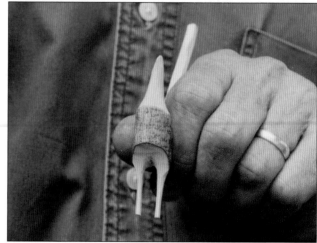

Step 9

Shape the top of the comb.

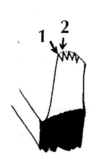

Note: *Especially on Steps 10, 11, 14 and 15, cut only a little at a time, making a (1) cut followed by a (2) cut, repeating these cuts as many times as necessary in order to get the desired shape. It's much better to make a number of shallow cuts than to dig in too deeply and end up splitting something you didn't mean to split!*

Step 10

Carve the front of the comb and the top of the beak. Sometimes I cut in a little under the front point of the rooster's comb—a style I've been following more recently in my own whittling history.

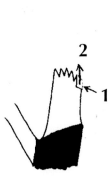

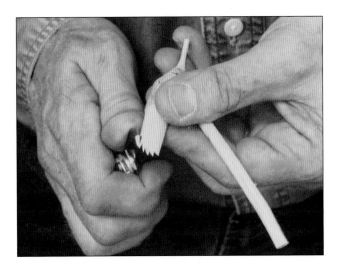

Step 11

Carve the back of the comb and the back of the neck.

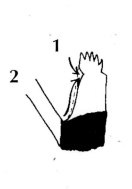

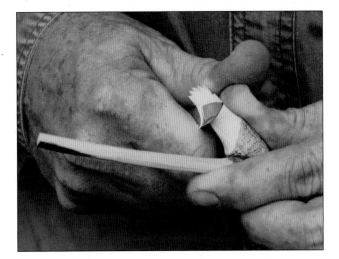

Step 12

Taper and sharpen the back point of the comb.

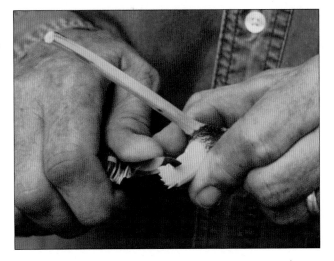

Note: *The order of Steps 12 and 13 can be reversed.*

Step 13

Sharpen the beak.

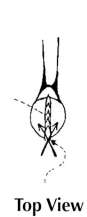

Top View

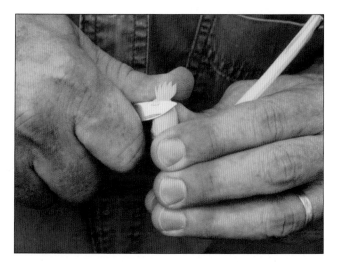

Step 14

Shape the beak.

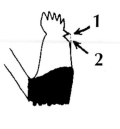

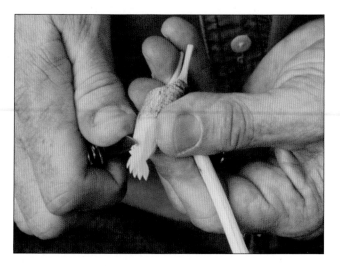

Step 15

Carve the wattles.

Step 16

Round and smooth the wattles and neck.

Step 17

Split the wattles by making a thin V-cut with the tip of the blade.

The completed rooster body.

Note: *If the wood fork you've been working with is fairly fresh, you'll probably need to hold off a bit before making the tail. How long you wait for the wood to dry depends on the thickness of the branch, how dry or humid the atmospheric conditions are, and what kind of wood you're using. If you made a test branch, try the tail cuts on the test branch first to see if the rooster branch is ready to cut.*

Rooster Tail

The next few steps look hard, but with practice they will become some of the easiest steps of all. Make sure your knife is sharp and follow the directions carefully.

To start, grip Branch C tightly and rest the rooster's chest and legs on a non-slippery surface. I tie my roosters to my left knee, just behind my kneecap with a belt or strap, or even a shoelace or piece of string. Tucking the rooster's legs under the strap will keep the rooster steady as you cut. Hold Branch C as you would a golf club and brace your forearms against your body for better stability and control.

Now, holding the larger blade almost flat against Branch C, make **short, repeated, forward-slicing motions** starting from point X. You may make as many

as six or eight, or even 10, of these little forward-slicing strokes to produce a feather. Be sure to cut each feather **all the way down to the same point** on the tail branch. Make each feather as thin as possible (especially the first half inch or so), starting each one a bit higher than the previous one until you get to point Y. Then cut each feather a little shorter until you "run out of wood" somewhere around point Z.

Finally, thin the base of the last feather with the small blade. Thinning the feather will allow you to bend it forward more easily. Always cut up, from the base of the feather to the tip, when you thin feathers. Spread the feathers into a "fan" using the flat part of the small blade.

Step 18

Make the tail.

Reminder: The feather stroke is a **short** stroke that can be **repeated** six or eight times on a single feather. It slices only on the **forward** stroke.

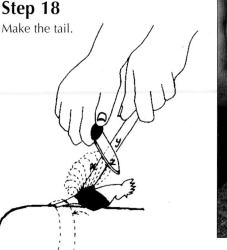

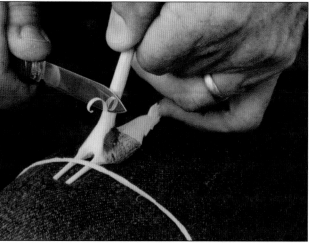

Slice the first feather. It is important to make this feather especially thin.

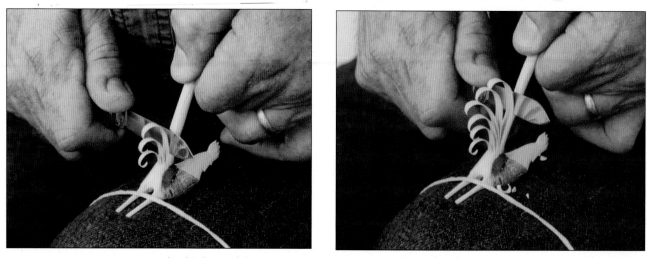

The feathers of the rooster's tail get progressively longer. The longest feather is cut at Point Y.

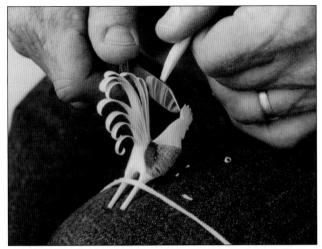

Make the final feathers successively shorter
until you run out of wood at point Z.

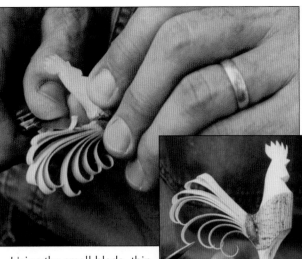

Using the small blade, thin
the base of the last feather in
order to bend it more easily.

Bend and fan the
feathers of the rooster's
tail into shape with the
flat side of the knife.
Don't be afraid to bend
the feathers. Because
they are carved with
the grain of the wood,
they are quite flexible.

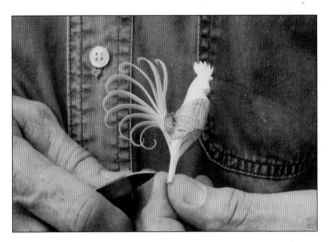

Painting and Finishing a Rooster

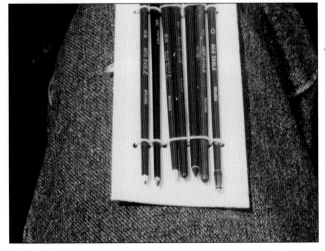

My collection of paintbrushes with sharpened handles.

Yellow	beak, legs
Red	comb, wattles
Black	eyes (Use a small, sharpened stick or the sharpened end of a brush handle.)

Paint the rooster with either acrylic or oil paints.
You'll be amazed at the difference a little bit of paint
makes on even a scruffy rooster. Make a base or stand

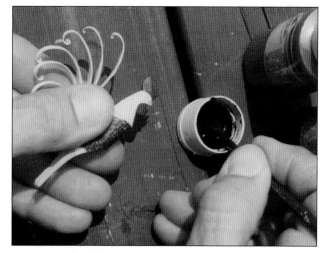

I always paint out of the lid so I can more easily control the amount of paint I am putting on the paintbrush.

Using the pointed end of the brush to paint the rooster's eye.

for the rooster. Using an awl or a sharpened nail, make holes for the rooster's legs. Glue the rooster in place, checking it from all sides to make sure it is standing straight. Your imagination can go a long, long way in placing your rooster on a unique stand or in a special setting. Finish the rooster with polyurethane, varnish or shellac. You don't need to finish the rooster, but a finish will protect the tail feathers.

One important word of caution: do not use a water-based polyurethane on your rooster. The water penetrates the thin, curled tail feathers and will straighten them out right before your eyes. You may want to try whatever clear finish you plan to use on a test curl to make sure it won't undo the nicely curled tail you've finished.

Just recently, Mike Shatt, a fellow branch-carver from Milford, Pennsylvania, shared a finishing tip with me. When he wants his little curls to retain their shape when painted with a water-based paint, he first coats the curls with liquid CA glue. When the glue dries, the curls are "petrified" and don't uncurl. While I've used CA glue to harden the thin curls for strength purposes, it never occurred to me to use the glue as a primer before using a water-based finish. Thanks for the tip, Mike.

The finished rooster mounted on a base.

Part of a twisted branch creates another simple setting for a rooster.

Choosing a Base

The base or setting into which you incorporate the figure you've just carved can make all the difference in the world. The variety is almost endless. Knotholes, gnarled pieces of bark, weathered stumps, chunks of firewood, vines...the list goes on. The following photos show a variety of base and setting ideas. Each base serves a different purpose or sets the rooster off in a different way. Over the years I've been absolutely amazed at some of the settings different people have made for their carvings.

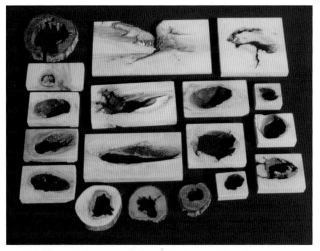

Knotholes and unusual natural formations in tree branches make unique bases and settings.

These are only some of the many materials on which you can set your finished carving.

This piece of bark makes a nice and simple setting for the rooster.

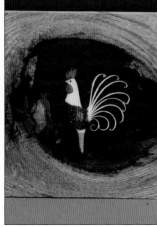

Placing your rooster in a knothole makes a unique framed piece.

What more appropriate place for a rooster than on a fence.

By adding a wreath and some string or ribbon, you can make your finished carving into a hanging ornament.

Hens and Chicks

I don't think I'll ever forget the encounter over thirty years ago when a lady, after looking over my display case of barnyard fowl, stated (72% good-naturedly, I think), "You're a chauvinist! All you have is roosters! *No hens?*" Well, it wasn't long before I figured out how to whittle hens too, if for no other reason than to put to rest that kind of commentary.

Since that day three decades ago, I've carved lots of hens, and baby chicks too (so as not to be accused of leaving the *kids* out). To be perfectly honest, however, I'll have to admit that I probably still carve about 10 to 20 roosters for every one hen I make. The main reason is that it takes a special fork to be a hen branch, while almost any half-decent forked branch will do for a rooster.

To make a good hen, both the top branches of the Y-fork need to be nearly the same diameter (sort-of like a good slingshot fork). The fork for a good rooster can have the much-more-common and easy-to-find thick/thin combination. The more symmetrical "hen fork" is definitely a more infrequent occurrence in nature and is much harder to find—hence, far fewer hens. See ladies, even in branch carving you are special!

Anyway, for those of you who would like to add some hens and chicks to your collection of branch carvings, here are a few suggestions.

While some of the carving strokes and techniques are similar, be sure to take note of some of the differences between the hen and the rooster:

- The hen's neck is shorter.
- Generally, the comb and wattles are smaller than those of the rooster.
- When you carve inward from the front and back of the bottom branch to make the legs (see step 3 on page 17), the cuts go in at a sharper angle and with a much more pronounced curve than the cuts on the rooster.
- Also, while the front cut for the rooster goes in deeper than the back cut, the front and back cuts on the hen are more equal.

Some other things to keep in mind:

- The hen's tail is formed by shaping the tail branch into a point.
- You can either leave the bark on the front of the hen, as you've done on the rooster, or you can take the bark off the front of the hen so that the remaining bark has more of a "wings" effect.

CHICK

- To make a hen sit on a nest, simply carve the hen without legs and place her in a nest of wood shavings, sawdust or dried grass.
- To add to the family, you can carve any number of baby chicks. The front and side drawings should give the idea of how to get the chick from the branch. Naturally, the setting in which you place the hen (and rooster and chicks) can vary greatly and add a lot to the creativeness and interest of the piece as a whole.

Tips for Correcting Splits and "Mess-ups"

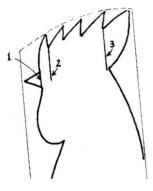

Figure A

Figure B: Correcting a split at line 1 (broken beak).

Figure C: Correcting a split at line 2.

Figure D: Correcting a split at line 3.

Figure E: Making a whole new head.

One of the great things about using twigs and branches as your main raw material is that you'll probably never go broke buying wood. The branches are free, and the only investment you have to make, outside of the time it takes to collect the branches, is the gas and shoe leather you use to get around.

Many times I'll find branches just lying on the side of the road, at construction sites, next to the curb on trash day or right in the backyard. You'd think that, with such a good supply of forks, whenever I make a mistake on a particular piece I could just throw the piece away and start over on a fresh branch. Hardly! Actually I doubt that I throw away more than six or eight "false starts" a year. It's rare that a branch-carving project can't be salvaged in some way or another.

One of the more common slips is in carving the rooster's head. This is especially the case when you're working with certain varieties of wood that are more brittle than others. So, what I'd like to do now is pass on a few of the ways I recover from overcuts, splits or other mess-ups on the rooster's head.

Figure A shows one of my average rooster heads. The three vertical lines (numbered 1, 2 and 3) show the three locations where a split occasionally occurs.

At this point, you could, of course, stop the carving process, glue the split, wait a while, and then continue. However, it's almost always faster and more practical to simply change the design a bit, give the rooster's head a slightly different shape, and just keep

going. After all, there are all different kinds of real roosters, and just think of all the different caricature possibilities.

The drawings in Figures B through E are fairly self-explanatory, I think. They just give corrective remake options, depending on where the split occurred or what piece broke off. Of course, don't forget that you can chop off the whole comb, or the entire head for that matter, and make a shorter, stockier variety of rooster. And if you totally mess up, you can always flip the rooster over, turn the legs into horns, glue on a couple of ears, paint on eyes, a nose and a mouth and, voilà, you have a goat or giraffe (sort of).

By the way, don't forget to sharpen the comb before making the comb cuts. (Step 8, page 20.) Doing so will enable you to make the comb more easily.

Just for fun, try different styles, shapes and proportions. Doing so will definitely keep you from getting into a rut, even if you specialize in just the rooster. There are tons of branches out there, to be sure, and it can be easy to give up on the one you're working on if it develops a problem. But a bit of experience has taught me that an unplanned split in a branch doesn't negate the branch's worth. Nor does it deny the possibility of a valuable piece of art emerging, even if the final shape is somewhat different from what I originally had in mind.

Pheasant, Heron and Roadrunner

I've never kept track of the number of branch carvings I've whittled since the summer of 1966…in the thousands, I'm sure. There's absolutely no doubt that the great majority of them have been roosters of all shapes and sizes and descriptions, but it has also been fun to add a few other figures and projects to the line.

I suspect that pheasants and herons are more or less tied for third place. (Hens would be in second….) At the time of this writing my guess is that I make one pheasant and heron for every 20 or 25 roosters. This is due in part to the fact that pheasant and heron "blanks" simply don't show up nearly as often as those that lend themselves to roosters, and also to the fact (at least in my case) that pheasants and herons take longer to make.

I definitely don't consider myself an expert on pheasants—not even branch fork pheasants. The techniques here work well for me, though you may want to refine them and develop your own techniques and detailing. Please feel free to do so, as a number of other carvers have done.

Four fine fowl: roadrunner, rooster, pheasant and heron.

Pheasant How-to

Because you don't want the pheasant's tail to curl, it's better to work with a branch that is quite fresh. The wetter the wood, the less the tail feathers will curl as you slice them. If you're working fairly fast and plan to finish the pheasant's body and tail in a relatively short time, you can go ahead and take the bark off the tail branch right away. However, if you think it's going to take you a while to get to carving the tail, wait until right before doing the tail to remove the bark. A de-barked tail branch will dry quicker than a tail branch with the bark intact. And remember, you'll need "wet" wood to get straighter, uncurled slices for the pheasant's tail.

Step 1

The ideal pheasant fork has a wider angle than most branch forks. You'll notice, too, that the pheasant fork is flipped upside down. When you cut the wood fork, leave the tail branch (Branch C) longer than you need for the finished tail.

Branch A
(head)

Branch B
(legs)

Branch C
(tail)

Step 2

Taper the sides of the head branch (Branch A) for the pheasant's head and neck. To leave enough bark for a "vest," make sure you don't start these cuts below the dotted line.

Step 3

Taper Branch B for the legs. Notice that the cuts are very curved and that more wood is taken from the front than from the back.

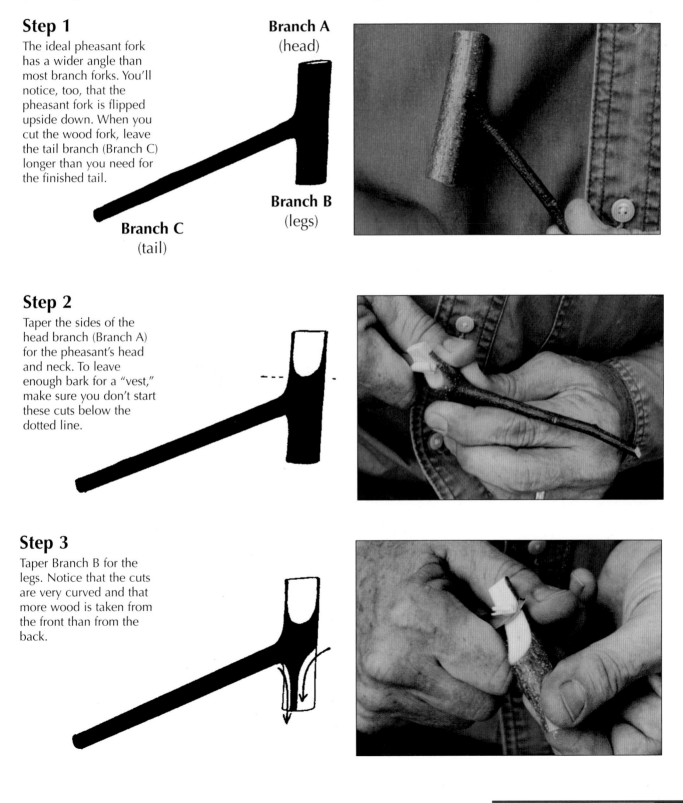

Step 4

Trim the bark to leave a natural bark "vest." Taper the head branch slightly. Take the bark and a little bit of wood off the outside of the legs, leaving some bark on the upper part of the legs. Remove the bark on the tail if you are finishing the pheasant right away; leave it on if you plan to carve the tail later.

Step 5

Now, cut out the legs. Begin at the point of the upside-down "V" and cut in the direction of the arrows. Make these cuts on both the front and the back. Then round and smooth the legs.

Start the cut here with the point of the blade.

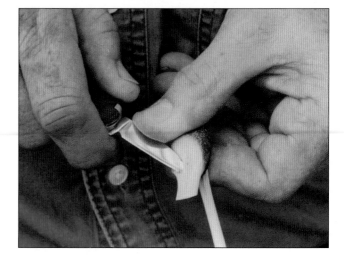

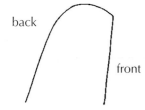

back

front

Step 6

Curve the top of Branch A.

Step 7

Cut the top of the beak and the top/front of the head.

Step 8

Round the sides of the top of the head. Sharpen the front to make the pointed beak.

Step 9

Carve the beak. Don't try to take the little "V" out in two cuts. Cut a little at a time, making a downward slanting cut followed by an upward slanting cut. Repeat this process several times until you get the beak shaped correctly.

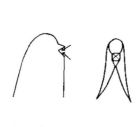

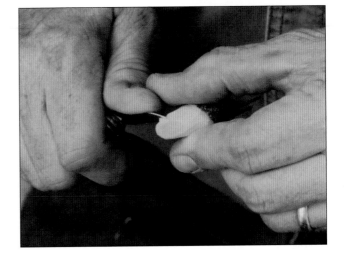

Step 10

Carve the bottom/front of the head and the front of the neck. Round the front and the back of the neck.

Pheasant Tail

If you're right-handed, place a belt, strap or string (whatever your portable vise happens to be) just above your left knee. If you're left-handed, place it above your right knee. I find that for the pheasant tail feathers it works better to use straight, pushing strokes down the branch, as opposed to the many repeated, short, forward-slicing strokes I generally use when doing the rooster tail. You'll notice in these photos that I am getting quite a bit of curl on my pheasant tail...actually quite a bit more curl than I want. (This is probably due to my branch being a bit drier than ideal when I started, or to my letting too much time pass between when I de-barked Branch C and when I started the tail slices.) In any case, it's not a serious problem. It's fairly easy to uncurl feathers after they're made. Just bend them straight with your fingers.

Step 11

As with the rooster, the knife blade needs to be very sharp. Remember to make the first feather especially thin. Thin the last tail feather, as shown in the photo on the right.

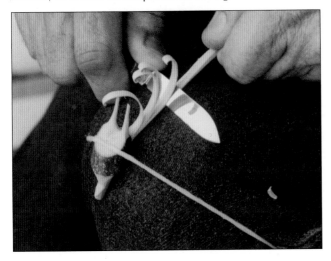

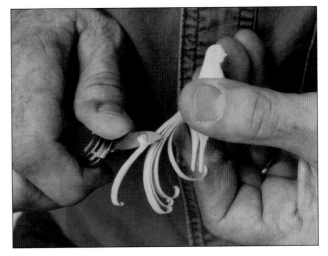

Step 12

There are a couple of ways to make these little neck feathers at the back of the head. a) The first way is to make several tiny tail-feather type cuts. b) The second way to make the feathers at the back of the head is to simply notch the head and the neck.

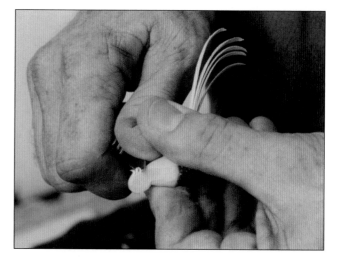

Step 13

You can really strengthen these delicate little feathers by letting a drop of liquid CA glue soak into them.

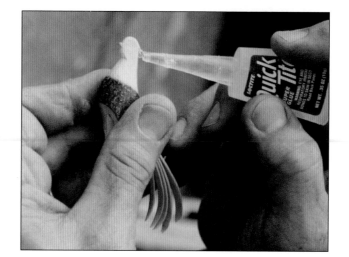

Paint the finished pheasant with acrylic or oil colors. I usually paint the beak and legs with the same yellow-orange as the rooster, but you may prefer another color. For the eyes, I use a four-step process in order to get a fairly realistic-looking eye. 1.) Paint a red diamond and let it dry. 2.) Paint a tiny black ball in the diamond. 3.) When the black ball is dry, paint a slightly smaller yellow ball in the center of the black ball. 4.) When the yellow ball is sufficiently dry, place a black dot in the very center. Presto! You have a very nice pheasant eye. (Minus the red diamond, you can do this eye on your other carvings as well.)

The finished pheasant.

Heron How-to

While I'm calling this particular bird a heron, I suppose it's really a sort of generic, long-legged, tall, slender waterfowl. You can call it an egret, too, or whatever else you decide to make it. The forks used for herons need to be straight-grained. The long A and B branches should be without knots. As with the pheasant, the heron fork is inverted.

Step 1

Cut the fork to size. Remember, it's important not to have knots that will weaken the legs or complicate the carving of the long, curved neck.

Note: *Not all woods lend themselves to herons as well as they do to roosters. Among those I've used successfully are maple, birch and wild cherry.*

Step 2

Taper Branch A for the head and the neck. Don't begin your cuts too low if you want the heron to have a natural bark "vest." An all-white, "barkless" heron looks good too.

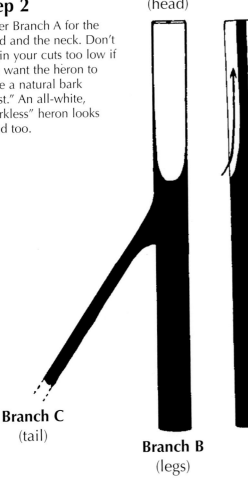

Branch A
(head)

Branch C
(tail)

Branch B
(legs)

Step 3

Taper Branch B to form the legs. Take more wood from the front than from the back.

Branch B
(legs)

Step 4

Trim the bark, leaving some to create the heron's natural vest. Take a little wood off the outsides of the legs as you remove the bark.

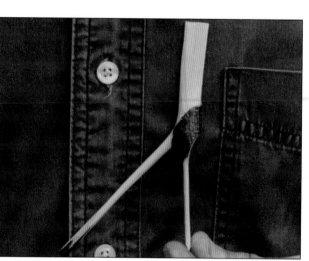

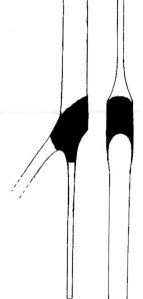

Step 5

Starting at the top of the legs and following in the direction of the arrows, cut out the legs. Make these cuts on both the front and the back. Very carefully round the legs. Go slowly. It's very easy to let your blade slice diagonally and cut off a leg!

Step 5 continued

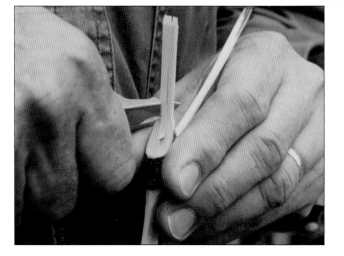

Step 5 complete

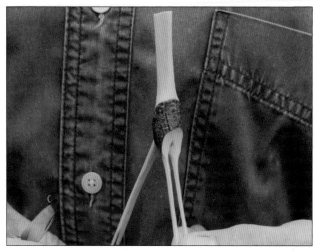

Step 6

Shape the heron's neck. Follow the arrows indicating the direction of the cuts. If you don't respect the direction of the grain, you'll end up cutting away more wood than you planned.

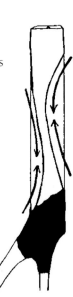

Step 7

Shape the head and the beak. Once again, watch the directions of these cuts. If you catch the grain the wrong way, it will be very easy to accidentally cut off the beak or even a good part of the head.

Step 7 continued

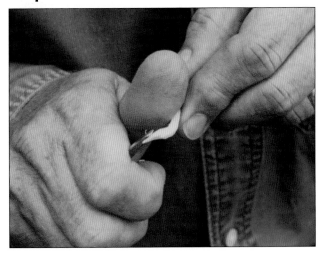

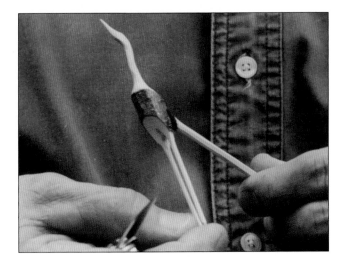

Heron Tail

Place the string "vise" around the heron's chest. Position the heron at the very end of your knee, even closer to the end of your knee than you positioned the rooster in Chapter Three. By positioning the heron so that the neck and head hang over your knee, you will be relieving some of the pressure that will be put on them as you make the tail slices.

The string below
shows the "vise."

Step 8

Make the feather cuts as you would on the rooster, starting with the shortest feather (the one closest to the back of the legs).

If it makes you a bit nervous to make this flat, slicing stroke over your knee, you might, as a precaution, want to place a piece of fabric or leather between the heron and your knee.

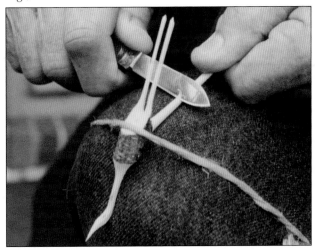

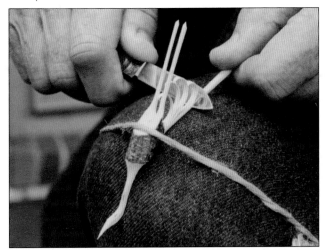

Step 9

After cutting through the tail branch, you'll most likely need to thin the last feather a bit. Always cut away from the heron's body toward the tip of the feather. Then separate and position the feathers as you want them.

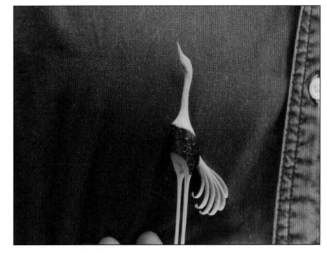

Step 10

Round and smooth the heron's head, beak, neck and legs. This is best done when the carving is dry and the wood has firmed up more. For this step you may want to use a tiny piece of fine sandpaper. Or, you can scrape these parts lightly with the knife blade, being careful not to lift the grain.

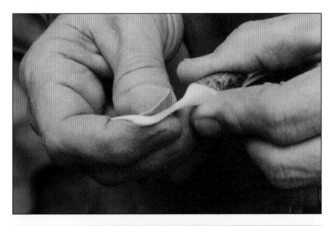

The finished heron.

Paint the heron and place it on a base. This particular bird ended up on a little piece of cottonwood bark. Driftwood and other unusually shaped branches and pieces of natural bark also make good settings and bases for water birds.

Roadrunner How-to

I rather doubt that any pure-blooded, self-respecting Southwest roadrunner would agree that it looks like the one that we're going to make here, but maybe the little guy that runs around in the cartoons, chased in every conceivable way by a certain coyote, will see a cousin!

The roadrunner requires a branch with two forks, one above the other. It's especially important that Branches C (tail), B (legs) and A (neck) are long, straight and without knots or extra branches. Branch E (beak) need not point straight ahead. It can be turned to one side or the other, or even backwards! The particular roadrunner illustrated in these photos is looking a bit to the left.

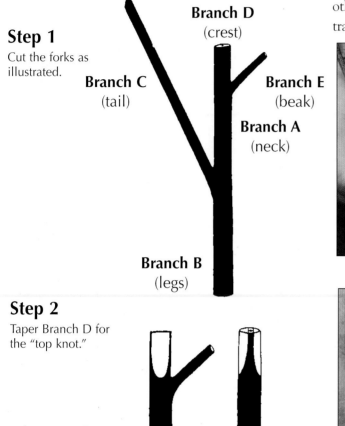

Step 1

Cut the forks as illustrated.

Branch D
(crest)

Branch C
(tail)

Branch E
(beak)

Branch A
(neck)

Branch B
(legs)

Step 2

Taper Branch D for the "top knot."

Step 3

Taper the sides of Branch E for the beak.

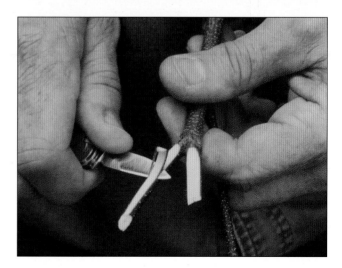

Step 4

Taper the sides of Branch A for the neck. Make sure to follow the direction of the arrows. Note where the cuts start and where the bark is left intact.

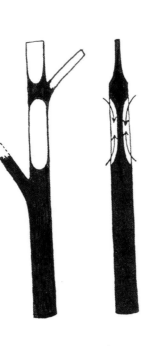

Step 5

Taper Branch B for the legs, taking more wood from the front than from the back. Make sure to get the curve at the top of these cuts so that the roadrunner's chest will stand out. Take the bark off the sides of Branch B. (Always remove the bark from the outsides of the legs before taking wood from between the two legs. That way you'll know just how much wood you have to work with when you carve the legs.)

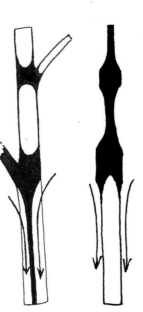

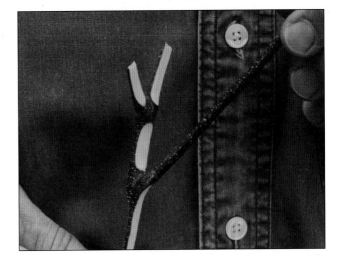

Step 6

Shape the top knot, the beak and the top of the head. Trim the bark to complete the top of the roadrunner's mask.

Step 7

Shape the front and the back of the roadrunner's neck. Round and smooth the neck and taper the bark neatly into the wood at the base of the neck where it joins the body and at the top of the neck where it joins the head.

Step 8

Cut out the legs. Do this very carefully in order not to lose control of the blade and slide diagonally through one of those thin legs!

Step 9

Cut out the eye holes in the mask. Make several notches in the top knot.

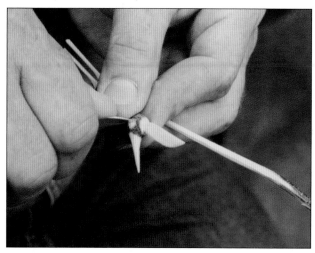

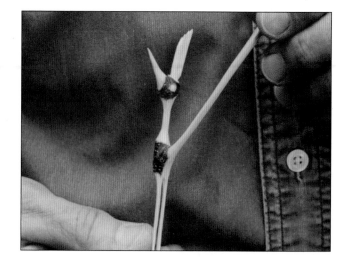

Roadrunner Tail

As with the rooster, pheasant and heron, you'll have much better control and precision if you tuck the roadrunner's legs under a string, belt or strap tied around your knee. I find I tend to make the roadrunner's tail feathers with a stroke that is somewhere between the one I use for the rooster and the one I use for the pheasant. The roadrunner's tail is quite long and shouldn't really have the curl that a rooster's tail has. It's all really a matter of practice, and by the time you've gotten this far, there's a good chance that you're already well along the way toward developing a technique with which you feel comfortable.

Step 10

Carve the roadrunner's tail.

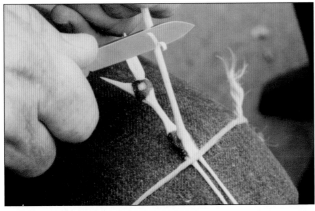
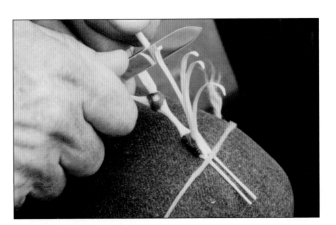
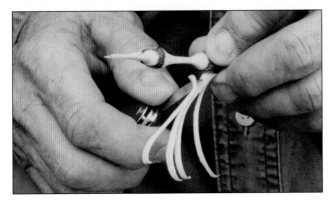

Step 11

Bend the tail feathers toward the back of the roadrunner's neck, positioning them however you think looks best. Smooth the legs and the neck with very fine sandpaper or by lightly scraping the surface with your knife blade.

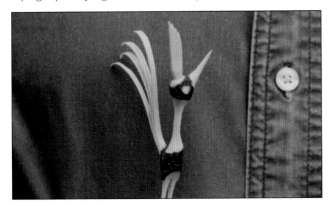

The finished roadrunner.

Paint the eyes, the beak and the legs. Apply finish. Mount the roadrunner on a base.

Miniature Trees and Flowers

The little trees I make are somewhat similar to ones that are found in Germany in that the branches and trunk come from a single piece. The German variety of trees that I've seen, however, have rings of branches that come into the trunk at the same level and are quite a bit larger than the little trees illustrated here. You'll notice that the branches on these miniature trees come down in a spiral.

Whittling a Tree

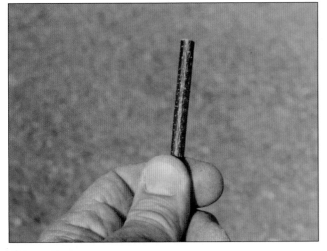

Step 1 Start with a straight little branch with no knots.

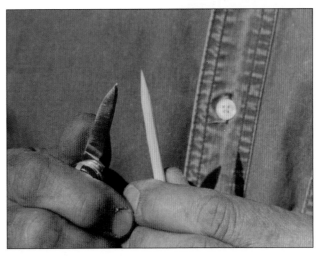

Step 2 Slice off the bark and taper the end of the branch to a symmetrical point.

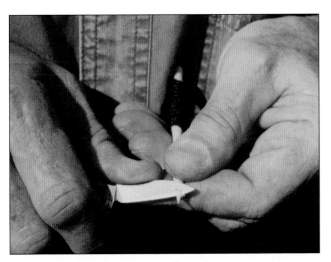

Step 3 With the thumb of the hand that's holding the blade resting against the finger(s) of the wood-holding hand, make very small, carefully controlled cuts toward the point of the stick.

Step 4 Each little branch will be the slightest bit longer than the preceding one.

Step 5 After each cut you'll turn the stick a little before slicing the next little branch. A right-handed carver will turn the stick clockwise, and a left-hander will turn it counter-clockwise.

Step 6 You can always tell if a right-hander or a left-hander carved the tree because of the direction of the corkscrew on the branches.

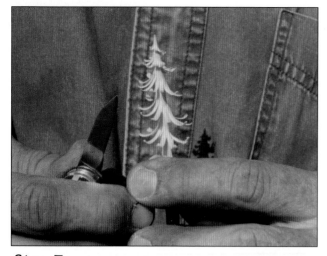

Step 7 At this point, if you want to stiffen the branches of the tree and reinforce them, you can wet them with liquid CA glue where they join the trunk of the tree.

Step 8 Trees that are done but not yet "planted."

Finished trees, planted on little chunks of bark. (Once or twice I've painted my trees green, but generally I've left them unpainted, just coated with a clear finish.)

The little flowers are made with a peeling down stroke, going around in a circle. Then I taper the stem to better match the size of the flower and leave enough wood to make a couple of little leaves.

Wildflowers and trees make great "habitat" material for roosters, herons, roadrunners and pheasants. Use oil-based paints to color the flowers; water-based paints will make the petals straighten and close.

Whittling a Flower

I'm quite sure there's been quite a bit written about how to whittle branch flowers by carvers who know more than I do. But, just for those of you who do not have those writings at hand, let me share some photos and comments on how I make my own particular brand of miniature flowers.

Step 1 Relatively straight branches of various diameters (from 1/16" to 1/4") work well for miniature flowers. I find that very fresh or wet branches tend not to make very open flower petals. Super-dry branches aren't good either, as the petals are brittle and break off easily. Something in-between fresh and dry is better to work with.

Step 2 Using long strokes, peel the bark off the branch. (Some folks like to leave the bark on the branch and make the first layer of petals with the bark.)

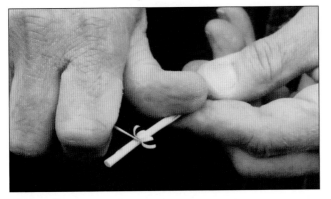

Step 3 With your thumb braced well below your cut, make thin, downward cuts for the petals.

Step 4 Depending on the thickness of the branch, you can make two, or even three or more, layers of petals. Try to position the petals of the succeeding layer in between the petals of the preceding one.

Step 5 When you're down to a little thin core that is too thin for another petal, twist it off.

Step 6 You're left with a little flower. Feel free to move the petals around a bit to position them as you'd like.

Step 7 Thin the stem to get it to a thickness proportionate to the size flower you have.

Step 8 The progress to this point.

Step 9 Cut downward to make a couple of leaves.

Step 10 Cut the flower off at the base of the stem.

Step 11 Now the flower is ready for painting. To keep the leaves and the petals from closing, I've almost always used oil-based enamel paint. As I mentioned before, Mike Shatt says that he can use water-based acrylics as long as he first brushes liquid CA glue on his petals and leaves. Any kind of thick bark makes a nice base for a bunch of flowers.

Whittling a Letter Opener

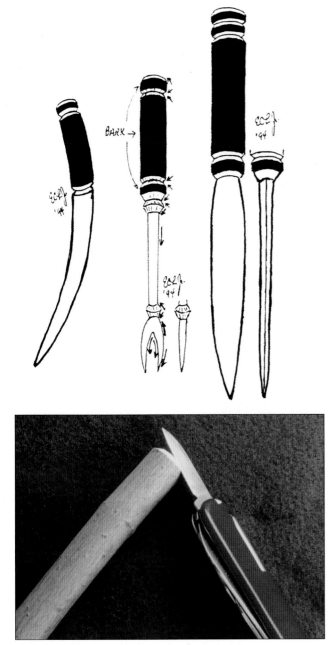

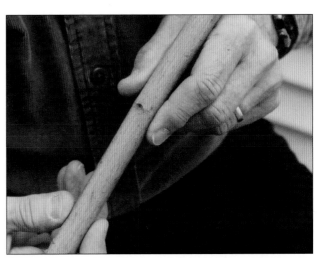

Step 1 Start by selecting a straight or slightly curved, relatively knot-free branch. Here, I've chosen a maple branch. For most of the rest of these steps, the hands will be invisible. That's because...Oh, it's way too long a story. Anyway, given the time constraints and the unavailability of my two photographers, I took the pictures myself. I'm sure you can figure out by now how to get the knife to make the particular steps and cuts illustrated.

Step 2 Round off the butt of the handle.

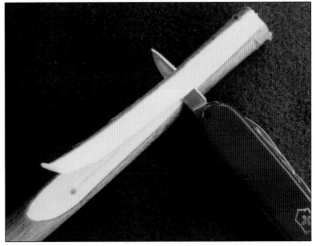

Step 3 Using long cutting strokes, taper both sides of the blade. Make sure you don't make the blade too thin. (Remember, you can always make it thinner later, but you can't glue wood back on after you've sliced it off.)

Step 4 Take just the bark off the back and the front of the blade.

Step 5 Chip out where the blade joins the handle.

Step 6 Make the upward curve on the bottom of the blade and a slight dip on the top, cutting toward the point.

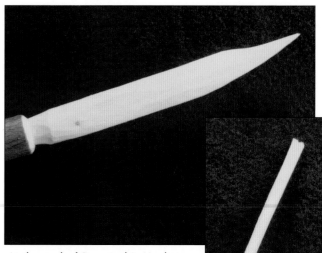

At the end of Step 6, this is what you have, seen from the side. The inset shows the top view.

Step 7 Sharpen the cutting edge of the blade. (If the wood you're working with is fairly fresh, don't make the blade too sharp at this point. Save your finer sharpening until the wood is drier and firmer.)

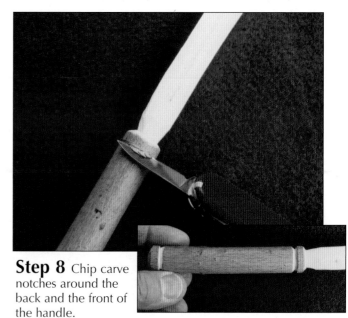

Step 8 Chip carve notches around the back and the front of the handle.

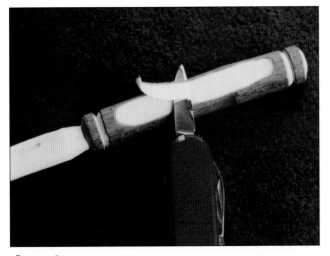

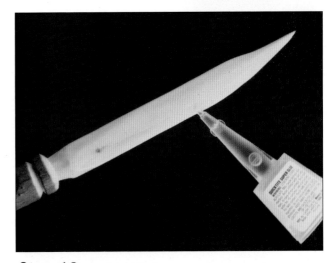

Step 9 If you wish, you can carve one or both sides of the handle. (Often I'll woodburn someone's name or some design.)

Step 10 Sand the blade into as sharp an edge as you'd like, and then run liquid CA glue along both sides of the cutting edge of the blade. When the CA glue dries, fine sand the blade again.

The finished letter opener seen from the bottom and both sides. Notice that the bottom view shows that the point is slightly off-center. The off-center point is intentional; it keeps the larger-than-desired pith from ending up on the sharp edge of the blade. If you look carefully at the one side view (the one with full bark on the handle), you'll see where I removed the soft pith and filled in the blade with a bit of wood filler. I'll almost always put on some type of clear finish at the end.

Several pieces of a chess set. Of course, the whole set has 32 pieces. From left to right: queen, king, pawn, bishop, knight and rook.

Corresponding pieces of the black set.

The chess board all set up and ready for some players. Dimensions of the chess board/table: 34" x 34". "Officially," when playing on this particular board, when you capture an opponent's piece, you must open one of the two little swinging gates and take the piece out *right*. Don't just unceremoniously pluck it up and over the rail fence!

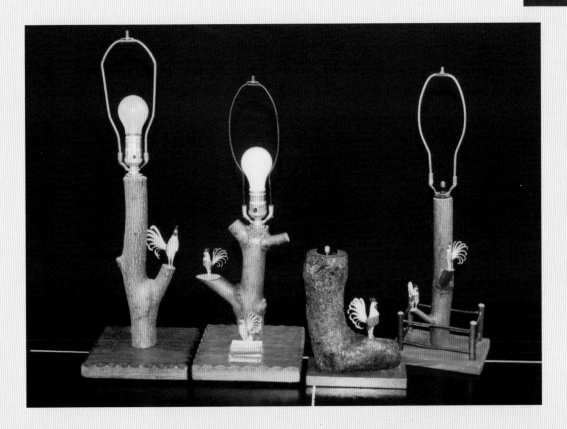

Branches of various shapes and pieces of firewood can be transformed into rather unusual and rustic lamps. The hardware and electrical components are easy to find.

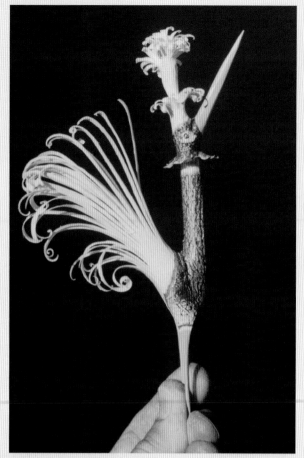

I haven't figured out a name for this one yet!

If you keep your eyes open for unusual branch formations, there's no telling what type of critter you can come up with. I have a feeling Dr. Seuss would approve of these!

A variety of kind of "funky" critters.

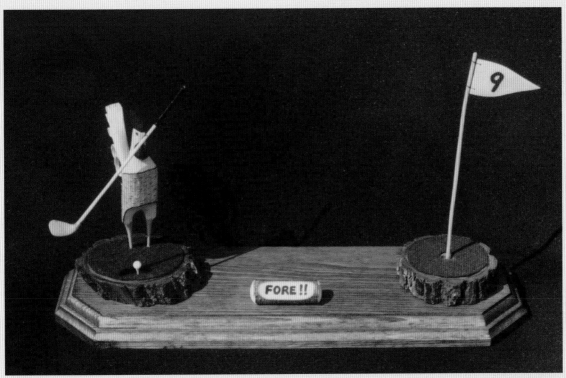

OK, so he's using a 5-iron for a very short hole...What would one expect a rooster to know about golf?!

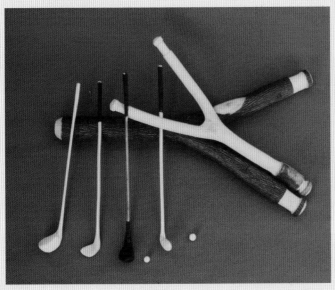

What you need for a golf club is a fork with a very thin but straight "shaft branch." Among the wood I've successfully used are birch, banyan and at least one variety of Florida oaks. For a pattern, just get ahold of a set of clubs. The basic shaping on all of the clubs is done with the knife, with the final smoothing and fine shaping done with a bit of sandpaper. The grip on the club can be either the bark itself or sewing thread wound around the shaft and held in place by a little carpenter's glue.

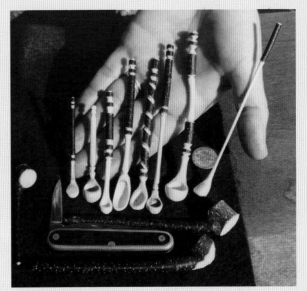

Miniature salt spoons and one lone golf club. The bowl of the little spoon on the left hasn't been hollowed out yet. To hollow out these spoons, I used a Dremel tool. The three branches at the bottom of the photo are "blanks" to be carved.

This eagle was carved from a symmetrical three-pronged fork, something that is very hard to find.

Talk about a rubbernecker!

Besides these sizes, branch-carved roosters can go a lot larger and a lot smaller.

One of these guys plays center on the barnyard fowl basketball team. The other is a starting defensive tackle on the poultry football team. Branch-carved roosters come in all shapes and sizes!

Over the years I've made a very limited number of "People" studies using differently shaped and positioned roosters to represent different human characters. This 21-piece set contains several species of branches. There's another set on the following page.

A couple with the kids.

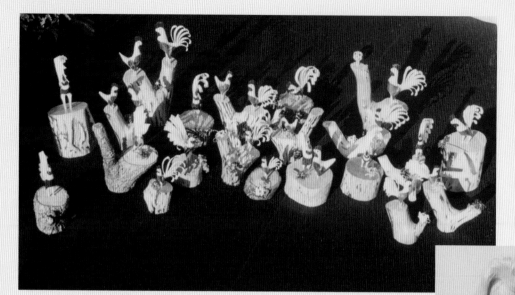

In my opinion, Shirley Smith, of Wommelsdorf, Pennsylvania, is one of the top branch carvers in the country.

I made this 20-rooster people study in Portugal.

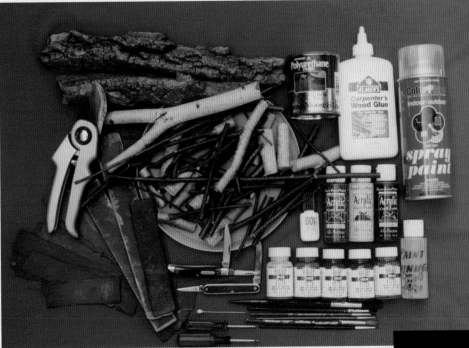

I wanted to see what I could make from just the branches, two pieces of cottonwood bark and the tools and supplies shown in the photo above. The other two photos show what resulted. The pile of chips is what was left over. And, also, I forgot to include in the above photo two other "tools" I used: a shoelace and a bit of sandpaper. Didn't want them to feel left out, so they're with the wood chips!

With some permanent markers and a little bit of woodburning, simple branch carvings become personalized desk plaques.

Rooster and hen pairs set in a variety of bases.

Adding a pen holder and a pen to this desk plaque makes it fun and functional. This piece sits on a desk in my doctor's office. The sign on the desk says, "The doctor is IN." No, I didn't carve the rooster's stethoscope. I purchased it at a doll miniature source.

A rooster and hen mounted on a base and accented with a woodburning tool and a bit of color can make a great wedding or anniversary gift (above and below left).

Branch "elbows" make nice arches.

I always enjoy making pieces for folks who want to honor or thank their parents in a special way.

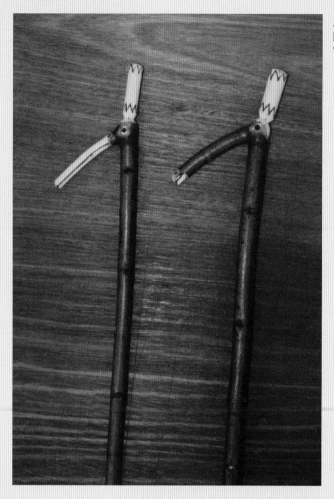

A couple of critter back-scratchers. Very easy to make!

Y-shaped branches can also be turned into quite a variety of birds other than the ones illustrated in the step-by-step demonstrations of this book.

Several heads: horse, woodpecker, goat and dog. The goat didn't start out to be a goat. It's a rooster that got messed up, the head chopped off, turned upside down, eyes cut in, ears glued on and *voilá*, a goat (sort of)!

A very intelligent, computer-literate rooster. The computer is carved from a branch, too.

Branch ostrich marionettes are all kinds of fun to make and use.

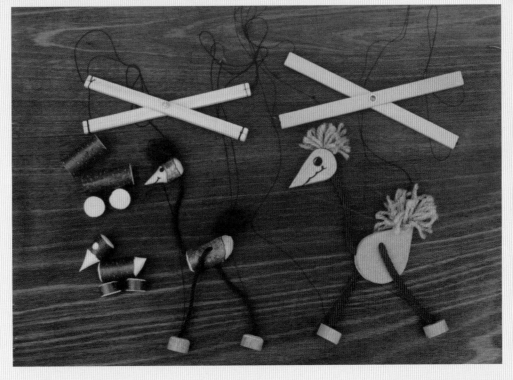

This handle, left natural, makes for an interesting and unique letter opener.

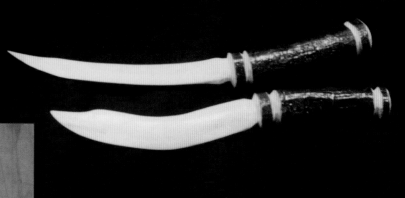

These letter openers were carved from pin oak branches that were cut down when I-295 was widened in southern New Jersey. The natural curves of the branches lent themselves to nicely shaped knives.

As seen here, letter openers can come in a variety of sizes.

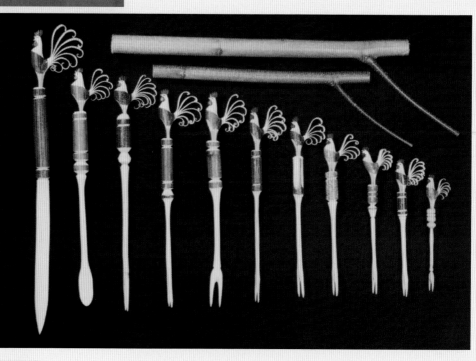

A collection of spoons, forks and knives topped with branch-carved roosters.

This large rooster is the biggest one I ever attempted with my little ICEL pocketknife. Here it is in process. The little dot in the glass box is the smallest rooster I ever carved with the same knife.

Years ago I showed my brother, Bill, a few how-tos of branch carving, and he, in turn, has passed on the ideas to friends in Brazil. Miguel Alves, a businessman from Anapolis, is one who has done some outstanding pieces.

Don Rannels of Lititz, Pennsylvania.

Many women have taken up branch and twig carving, too. I admire this woman's work, but I'm embarrassed that I lost the paper with her name.

Ed Easterwood, a Florida carver, shows his creations—including several branch-carved roosters—at a carving show.

Some young carvers have done great jobs!

One of the workshop groups in Bismarck, North Dakota. Here's hoping you'll have lots of fun adding portraits of your own branch carvings to this gallery.

More Great Project Books from Fox Chapel Publishing

The Little Book of Whittling
Passing Time on the Trail, on the Porch, and Under the Stars
By Chris Lubkemann

Learn to whittle a knife, spoon, goat head, canoe and more. Makes a great gift.

ISBN: 978-1-56523-274-7
$12.95 · 104 Pages

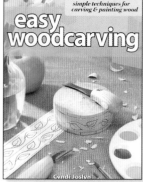

Easy Woodcarving
Simple Techniques for Carving and Painting Wood
By Cyndi Joslyn

All a new woodcarver needs to get started. No previous carving knowledge necessary. This book teaches the basics of carving with the easy-to-follow skill-building exercises and hundreds of color photos.

ISBN: 978-1-56523-288-4
$14.95 · 152 Pages

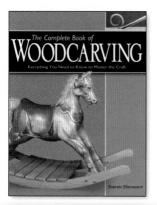

Complete Book of Woodcarving
Everything You Need to Know to Master the Craft
By Everett Ellenwood

Comprehensive reference covers every classic style, along with power carving. Also contains 9 projects and helpful resource section.

ISBN: 978-1-56523-292-1
$27.95 · 288 Pages

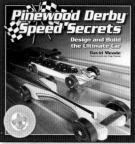

Pinewood Derby Speed Secrets
Design and Build the Ultimate Car
By David Meade

Hundreds of photos and diagrams for making the fastest Pinewood Derby car in the race. Written by an undefeated derby champ. This book has everything you need to take home the prize.

ISBN: 978-1-56523-291-4
$12.95 · 120 Pages

Kid Crafts: Woodworking
From the Kid Crafts Series
By John Kelsey

Discover the fun of woodworking with 10 projects that only require ordinary lumber and simple hand tools. Learn to build a bird nesting box, tool box, and much more.

ISBN 978-1-56523-353-9
$12.95 · 104 Pages

Pinewood Derby Designs & Patterns
The Ultimate Guide to Creating the Coolest Car
By Troy Thorne

Build the coolest car with jaw-dropping designs from a derby-winning dad. Learn techniques for increasing speed, and making your own decals. This handy manual includes patterns for a High-Wing Racer, a Stock Car, Army Jeep and more.

ISBN: 978-1-56523-341-6
$12.95 · 128 Pages

WOODCARVING
ILLUSTRATED

In addition to being a leading source of woodworking books and DVDs, Fox Chapel also publishes Woodcarving Illustrated. Released quarterly, it delivers premium projects, expert tips and techniques from today's finest carvers, and in-depth information about the latest tools, equipment, & materials.

Subscribe Today!
Woodcarving Illustrated: **888-506-6630**
www.WoodcarvingIllustrated.com